J 934 Cle
Clements, Gillian
Indus Valley city

$28.50
ocn213306420
08/26/2009

D1087264

Building History
INDUS VALLEY CITY

Gillian Clements

SEA-TO-SEA
Mankato Collingwood London

This edition first published in 2009 by Sea-to-Sea Publications
Distributed by Black Rabbit Books
P.O. Box 3263
Mankato, Minnesota 56002

Printed in China

Library of Congress Cataloging-in-Publication Data:

Clements, Gillian.
  Indus Valley city / Gillian Clements.
      p. cm. -- (Building history)
  Includes index.
  Summary: "Discusses the Indus Valley civilization of Southeast Asia, including what
archaeological evidence tells us about their customs and how they built their cities"--
Provided by publisher.
  ISBN 978-1-59771-144-9
  1. Indus civilization--Juvenile literature. I. Title.
  DS425.C583 2009
  934--dc22

                              2008004577

9 8 7 6 5 4 3 2

Published by arrangement with the
Watts Publishing Group Ltd, London.

Editor: Sally Luck
Art Director: Jonathan Hair
Consultant: Dr. Justin Morris,
Curator of South Asian Archaeology,
The British Museum, London

Contents

6-7   What was an Indus Valley city?

8-9   Who discovered the Indus cities?

10-11   Why build near a river?

12-13   Who were the Indus people?

14-15   Why did their cities grow?

16-17   How was an Indus city planned?

18-19   How did they build the cities?

20-21   What was city life like?

22-23   What was it like inside a house?

24-25   How has the Indus culture continued?

26-27   What happened to the Indus cities?

28   Timeline

29   Glossary

30   Index

What was an Indus Valley city?

Four-and-a-half thousand years ago, a civilization flourished in the valley surrounding the Indus River, in Southern Asia. It was the ancient world's largest civilization but, until recently, it remained undiscovered—buried under the ground.

What is a civilization?

The word "civilization" refers to a large, organized group of people with a shared culture. Unlike most people who lived thousands of years ago, the Indus people were not traveling hunters. They came together to live in villages, towns, and cities, with laws and rules; they formed a civilization.

Where were the Indus cities?

In the 1920s, archeologists were digging in the Indus Valley in Northwest India (in an area which later became Pakistan). They discovered two remarkable cities, Mohenjo-daro and Harappa. The two cities were a long way apart—350 miles (563km)—but were very alike. Both had a higher, walled area (called a citadel) and a lower area beneath, with hundreds of houses.

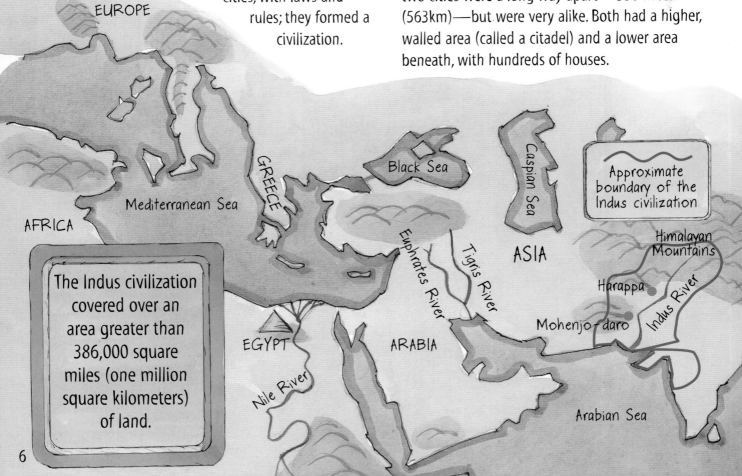

The Indus civilization covered over an area greater than 386,000 square miles (one million square kilometers) of land.

Approximate boundary of the Indus civilization

EUROPE

AFRICA

Mediterranean Sea

GREECE

Black Sea

Caspian Sea

ASIA

Himalayan Mountains

Euphrates River

Tigris River

Harappa

Indus River

Mohenjo-daro

EGYPT

ARABIA

Nile River

Arabian Sea

3300 B.C.E	3300–2800 B.C.E	2600–2500 B.C.E	1900–1700 B.C.E
Mohenjo-daro and Harappa are riverside farming villages.	People farming in the area begin to form larger settlements.	Indus civilization grows and spreads. Craftsmanship and trade help towns and cities develop.	The Indus civilization ends. Small local cultures replace it.

When did the civilization flourish?

The Indus civilization began around 2600 B.C.E. At this time, people in the Indus area began making a new kind of pottery and started a new religion. These changes helped bring about the rise and success of the Indus civilization. In the centuries between 2600 and 1900 B.C.E. the culture grew, flourished, and then seemed to disappear.

Indus ▶ jewelry, pottery, and seals

Where did the Indus people live?

Many people lived in the Indus cities. However, thousands more lived in villages and towns around the Indus River, and other important rivers. Some people lived in trading outposts, south at the coast or north in the foothills of the Himalayan Mountains. These settlements were a long way from the cities and were used by traveling traders.

An Indus priest

Who built the cities?

The evidence found by archeologists suggests that religious leaders or merchants planned the layout of the cities. They would then have organized villagers and townspeople into gangs of laborers to carry out the building work.

An area of houses inside an Indus Valley city ▶

Who discovered the Indus cities?

Some local Indian legends told of an ancient city in the Punjab district. However, few people realized there was a great civilization beneath their feet! Sir Alexander Cunningham was the first archeologist to excavate the area.

 Sir Alexander Cunningham was an important British archeologist working in India at the end of the 19th century, when India was part of the British Empire. When local people from the Harappa area found strange brick ruins, Cunningham thought they were only a few years old and probably from a Buddhist temple. However, in his first Harappa excavation (1872-73) he found no temples—just pottery, and a mysterious stamp seal.

British people living in India considered some parts of the country to be wild and uncivilized. They did not believe that a complex civilization had existed in the Punjab, thousands of years before. They were wrong!

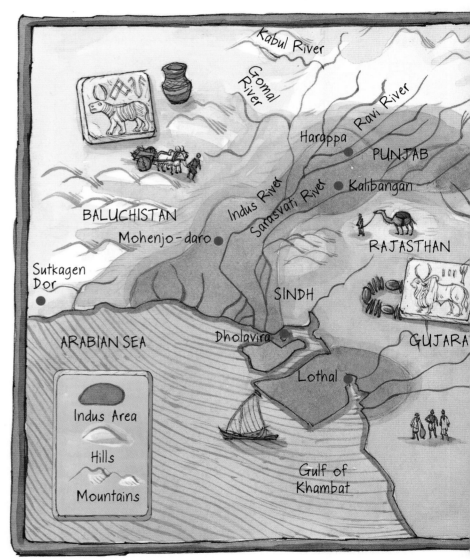

Sir John Marshall was the British director of the Archeological Survey of India in the 1920s. In 1924, his excavations revealed a huge citadel platform at Mohenjo-daro. He then announced the discovery of the unknown Indus civilization.

Rakal Das Banerji was the Superintending Archeologist of the Western Circle. He excavated in 1919 and found Indus seals.

Bahadur Daya Ram Sahni excavated at Harappa in 1920 and 1921. He found more seals with different words and pictures.

George Dales & Mark Kenoyer excavated Harappa in 1986 and discovered more about Indus craftsmen and merchants.

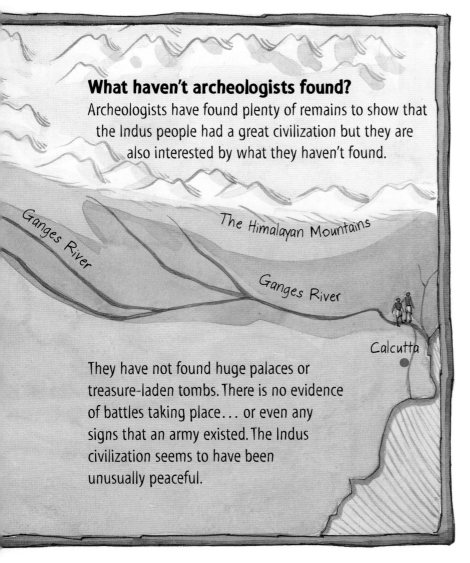

What haven't archeologists found?

Archeologists have found plenty of remains to show that the Indus people had a great civilization but they are also interested by what they haven't found.

Ganges River

The Himalayan Mountains

Ganges River

Calcutta

They have not found huge palaces or treasure-laden tombs. There is no evidence of battles taking place... or even any signs that an army existed. The Indus civilization seems to have been unusually peaceful.

How do archeologists find out about the past?

Archeologists often have to dig through layers in the ground to find out about the past. Each layer represents a "living surface," on which people have lived and built their homes. After many years, buildings fall down and the ground flattens. Each time this happens, new homes are built and the "living surface" level becomes higher. Archeologists can date each level by identifying the buildings, pottery, coins, and other artifacts they find there.

▲ Diagram showing "living surface" layers

Archeological work has continued in the Indus area ever since the first big excavations.

Why build near a river?

Harappa, the great city of the Upper Indus region, was built next to the Ravi River. Mohenjo-daro, in the Lower Indus region, was on the right bank of the Indus. There were many reasons for building near a river.

Water for ceremonies

The Great Bath, in Mohenjo-daro's citadel, was probably used for worshippers to clean themselves during religious ceremonies. It had to be built near a river to get a good supply of water.

In the 1970s, it was discovered there were as many settlements along the sacred Sarasvati River as there were along the Indus. For this reason, the civilization is sometimes called the Indus-Sarasvati civilization.

Ganweriwala

INDUS RIVER

Mohenjo-daro

Chanhu-daro

Water for farming

The Indus River was at its lowest level in winter and highest in midsummer. Barley and wheat were sow just after the midsummer floods and they grew well, even without plowing and irrigation. Other crops needed river irrigation.

Sofka Koh

Dholavira

ARABIAN SEA

River trade and communications

Trade was very important to the huge Indus culture. Bullock carts made good overland vehicles, if the land was flat. However, traveling by river and sea was the fastest and easiest way to take goods to faraway markets.

Harappa

Kalibangan

RAVI RIVER

SARASVATI RIVER

Nile River

EGYPT

Egypt

Ancient Egypt's civilization grew up along the River Nile, where the land was fertile for farming. Cities, towns, and the famous pyramids were built along its banks, and builders and traders relied on it to transport stone and goods.

Water supply and waste disposal

Keeping cities clean was very important to the Indus people. Waste water in city drains and sewers was channeled away from the cities, out toward the rivers. There was also a good supply of water to public and private wells.

Euphrates River

Tigris River

MESOPOTAMIA

Mesopotamia

This area is sometimes called "the cradle of civilization," because it is where the first cities were built. The land between the Tigris and Euphrates rivers was good for farming. The area became home to the ancient Sumerian and Assyrian cultures.

Fishing

Indus people ate a lot of fish. They fished for carp in the rivers and for a variety of fish in the sea. Living near a river gave people a good food supply.

Who were the Indus people?

It is difficult for us to find out a lot about the Indus people, because we can't understand their writing. We have to look at archeological evidence to try to learn about them.

What did they look like?

Indus sculptures of women

Hairstyles

Stone and clay Indus sculptures show us that men had a variety of hairstyles. Some women had simple braids but others had intricate hairstyles, or wore hats. Their clothes varied too, and this probably depended on their job or their place in society.

The famous "Priest King" sculpture

An Indus farmer

Jewelry

Indus people wore a lot of jewelry, such as bangles and necklaces. Craftsmen were skilled at making beads from different kinds of stone. As with clothing, the type of jewelry people wore may have shown their place in society.

What did they believe?

Water ceremonies

The cleanliness of the cities and the Great Bath of Mohenjo-daro suggest that water was an important part of Indus religion. Water is also very important in Hinduism, one of the major religions in India today.

Shells, used as water vessels in ceremonies

Burials

In the grave sites in Harappa, Lothal, and Kalibangan, bodies have been found buried with pottery and other personal items. This suggests Indus people believed in an afterlife which, again, probably linked into religious beliefs.

Pottery found in graves

This seal might show a marriage procession of the gods.

Religious seals

Many Indus seals show pictures of gods, which indicates how important religion was to them. Plants, trees, and animals also feature. These are important in the Hindu religion today and many archeologists believe elements of this may link back to the Indus culture (see pages 24-25).

What did the Indus people do?

Farmers grew a great variety of crops such as barley, wheat, rice, chickpeas, field peas, mustard, sesame, grapes, dates, melons, and cotton. They also raised animals such as cattle, water buffalo, sheep, goats, pigs, chickens, dogs, and camels.

Traders used seals to identify their trade goods. Many Indus people were traders. Seals from the Indus Valley have been found as far away as Mesopotamia, Central Asia, Iran, and Afghanistan. This tells us that traders traveled far to sell their goods.

Craftsmen made things for people to use in their homes, such as pottery and tools. These goods were also traded, as were luxury items. Gemstones, such as cornelian and lapis lazuli, became beautiful beaded jewelry in the skilled hands of the Indus craftsmen.

Priests played an important part in ruling the civilization. There would probably have been a major priest in each town or city, who acted as a local ruler. Other priests may have collected goods from the public, both for taxes and for making offerings to the gods.

Women The clay and stone figurines show us what women might have looked like, but we can only guess at what their daily activities were. Women were most probably involved in running the household, but could they have had jobs outside the home too?

Why did their cities grow?

The Indus cities grew for two main reasons; the people had clever business minds, and there were excellent river, coastal and overland trade routes.

Area in which Indus people traveled to trade

How did trade routes help the cities grow?

Traders and craftsmen used the trade routes to bring raw materials (from the Indus area and farther afield) into the towns and cities, where they were turned into jewelry, pottery, and metalware. Such goods were very valuable and helped the cities prosper and grow.

WEST:
Indus traders traveled to Mesopotamia and Persia by land and, more usually, by sea.

How did the Indus traders travel around?

Long, flat-bottomed ferryboats were used to carry people and goods by river. However, to travel to places like Mesopotamia and Persia (modern Iran), it was quicker to sail in strong sea boats up the Persian Gulf. On land, Indus traders used bullock carts.

Did the Indus people trade in Mesopotamia?

The Mesopotamians wrote about importing goods from the Indus people. Their texts mention gold, copper, lapis lazuli, and wood. The fact that archeologists have found Indus seals and other artifacts in Mesopotamia proves Indus people traded there.

NORTH:
Indus traders traveled north as far as Central Asia looking for jade to make jewelry. Nearer to the Indus area, in Afghanistan, they bought gold and lapis lazuli.

Harappa

Kalibangan

Ganweriwala

Mohenjo-daro

Chanhu-daro

Dholavira

Lothal

	Major trade routes
	Cornelian
	Timber
	Shell
	Fish
	Copper
	Gold
	Silver
	Flint
	Steatite
	Turquoise
	Amethyst
	Alabaster
	Jade
	Lapis lazuli

SOUTH:
Indus traders traveled by bullock cart, or sailed down the coast to reach southern trading posts. They traded for cornelian in Gujarat, and amethyst farther south in Maharashtra. Both of these could be made into beads.

It is hard to work out how many people lived in each of the Indus cities. Some historians think, at its largest, Harappa's population was as high as 80,000 people.

How was an Indus city planned?

When archeologists excavated mysterious brick and earth mounds around the Indus area, they found rectangular cities and towns, laid out in an orderly grid pattern.

This map shows the excavation site at Mohenjo-daro, as found by Marshall's team (see page 8)

The citadel and the lower city

Big Indus cities like Mohenjo-daro and Harappa had two main parts: a high-walled citadel to the west and a lower city to the east. At Mohenjo-daro, archeologists discovered a street grid dividing the city into 12 blocks of houses.

The area of the Mohenjo-daro citadel

Granary

Great Bath

College

Pillared hall

Remains of citadel wall

Mohenjo-daro's citadel

The citadel was surrounded by 19-foot (6m) high walls and had mostly civic and religious buildings inside. Some religious leaders may have lived there too. To enter the sacred area, visitors had to climb a tall flight of stairs and pass through a bathing place where they may have had to wash to purify themselves.

Like the Egyptians, Indus people used their knowledge of the heavens to find true north. From that, they were able to line up their city streets north-south, east-west.

The North Star!

Were the granaries really granaries?

For a long time, experts thought that hall-like buildings in citadels were granaries, for storing grain. These buildings were built on blocks to allow the air to flow underneath, just like the ancient Roman granaries. However, no traces of grain have been found and archeologists now wonder if these granaries were actually palaces.

The granary at Mohenjo-daro

A street plan in the city

An Indus house

Fields outside the Indus cities were plowed for farming.

The area of the lower city

The lower city

The brick houses of Mohenjo-daro's lower city were built in orderly rows and blocks, nestled in a maze of streets and narrow alleyways that branched off bigger main streets. Most Indus houses were a standard size, but some neighborhoods had big, luxurious houses for wealthy people, such as merchants and landowners.

The road leading to the citadel

Local farmers

How did they build the cities?

Builders used materials that they found locally. Most bricks were made from mud, which was easy to find all along the riverbanks.

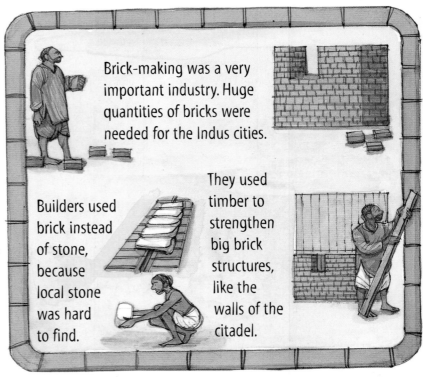

Brick-making was a very important industry. Huge quantities of bricks were needed for the Indus cities.

Builders used brick instead of stone, because local stone was hard to find.

They used timber to strengthen big brick structures, like the walls of the citadel.

What tools did they use?

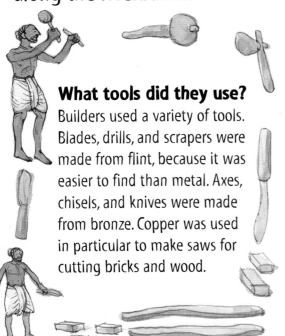

Builders used a variety of tools. Blades, drills, and scrapers were made from flint, because it was easier to find than metal. Axes, chisels, and knives were made from bronze. Copper was used in particular to make saws for cutting bricks and wood.

How did they make the bricks?

Brick-makers made most of their bricks to a standard size. The uniform size and shape made Indus city walls and buildings look really impressive.

Brick-makers filled wooden molds with mud, and left them to dry out.

The bricks were tipped out of their molds and stacked.

Bricks were baked hard in the Sun or in an oven for extra strength.

A few bricks were sawn to a particular size.

Citadel walls were often many yards thick.

The bricks were laid in a special "bond," which made a long and short pattern.

How did they build the Great Bath?

Builders had to make the base and sides of the Bath completely watertight. They did this by sandwiching a substance called bitumen tar between layers of specially sawn bricks. When the builders had finished building the Bath, they built raised columns on the Bath's north, east and south sides.

Brick

Bitumen

Brick

How was the Great Bath supplied with water?

A large well supplied the Great Bath with water. The water could then be drained through a corner outlet into a bigger drain, and away out of the city.

In all the Indus cities, the standard brick size was 3in x 5.5in x 11in (7cm x 14cm x 28cm), a ratio of 1:2:4.

A brick alleyway in the lower city

Cross-section of a well

How did they control the city's water?

Indus cities had public and private wells, and drains from all the lower city's houses. These fed into street drains, and then into even bigger drains which ran along the center of most main streets.

What was city life like?

The Indus cities would have been peaceful places to live, controlled by priests, merchants, and landowners.

How did religion affect city life?

Religious ceremonies were a big part of city life and they normally took place in the citadels. Priests may have held sacred bathing ceremonies at the Great Bath at Mohenjo-daro. Not far away archeologists have found a statue lying in an oblong, colonnaded building. This is thought to have been a temple for religious worship.

▲ The Great Bath at Mohenjo-daro

▲ The granary at Mohenjo-daro

How did traders pass in and out of the city?

Most Indus cities had carefully located entrances in the thick walls. Some were narrow but others were wide enough for a bullock cart to pass through. As traders passed in and out, city officials may have taxed them and their goods. They would have used stone seals pressed into clay tabs to mark the goods.

The distinctive Indus seals were pressed into wet clay, to form clay tabs. They left a raised impression— normally of some writing with a picture below.

What happened in the lower city?

Most people lived in the lower city, east of the citadel. Archeologists have found Indus homes and workshops side by side here. The homes came in different sizes. This shows that there were probably different layers of society: the rich and the not so rich.

What happened in the craft workshops?

Craftsmen made seals from gray steatite stone. They were cut and carved with a copper tool.

Making etched cornelian and long-barreled beads required great skill. Beads were also made from materials such as clay, stone, shell, and ivory.

Archeologists have found cotton bags and cotton fishing lines. Raw cotton bales must have been spun, woven, and dyed in the lower city.

Clay was used to make different kinds of pottery. Some pots were made to hold seals, beads, and jewelry.

Most pots were made on pottery wheels, then fired (baked) and decorated with red slip (runny clay) and black patterns.

Death in the city

Indus people were buried with personal items, which suggests they believed in an afterlife. However, they weren't wasteful people and they didn't bury precious items with their dead.

Experts have studied the bones of people buried in the cities. They can tell that, in life, these people were well fed and healthy. Poorer people may have been cremated or have had river burials.

What was it like inside a house?

The Indus mud-brick city houses had high ceilings and thick walls, to keep them cool in the heat of the day. Some houses had just one room, with a bathing area partitioned off. But rich people had large homes with several rooms, a courtyard and an upper floor.

Householders could relax in the Sun on a brick platform outside the house, or work in the shade of a tree.

This fish looks tasty!

The kitchen had a hearth, and was in one of the outer rooms.

Windows let in light and air. Some may have had wooden or stone lattice grilles, and wooden shutters.

The living room may have been used as a workshop, where beads, stone tools, pots, and other household artifacts were made.

People entered their homes from a side lane. Walls next to the main streets had no doors or windows, for peace and privacy.

See you at lunch!

The city was kept free of litter. Workmen cleared garbage from cans built on the sides of houses.

The upper floor was used for stores and for personal rooms.

Did people work in their homes?
Experts think some people had workshop areas in their home—in the courtyard or in the living room. However, they have also found buildings which seem like separate workshops. These were in the same part of town as the houses.

The flat roof was made using strong wooden beams, filled in with matting and plaster. People worked, relaxed, and slept there in the open air.

Waste water drained into the sewer.

The well

How were the houses supplied with water?
Many city homes had private wells, latrines, and bathrooms. The best bathrooms had watertight brickwork on the floors and in the drains. The water system was very efficient for its time. Open waste drains led out through pipes and chutes to street drains—and eventually to city sewers.

Brick stairs led to upstairs rooms and the flat roof.

The courtyard was a quiet place for work (including weaving and washing clothes) and for relaxation. Children could play there in safety.

The Indus people may have lived as far back as 2800 B.C.E. However, some aspects of their culture have survived and are still part of life in India and Pakistan today.

This Indus seal shows an elephant. Hindus worship the elephant god, Ganesha.

Religion

Indus seals often have pictures of bulls, tigers, elephants, tree-spirits, and of gods who are seated cross-legged. In fact Indus people and modernday Hindus seem to share some gods and goddesses, and honor the same animals and trees.

The cow and bull

The cow and bull are sacred to Hindus, as symbols of fertility and prosperity. Historians believe they were sacred to the Indus people, possibly for the same reasons.

The area where the Indus people lived is now largely Muslim. However, it is the Hindu religion that has carried forward some of the Indus culture.

The Hindu Goddess Shiva (left) is like the figure shown on the Indus seal (below).

Elephant head figurine, found in Harappa

Script and language

Experts believe the Dravidian language of the Indus people is similar to the one spoken today in the south of India, particularly by the Tamils.

Society

Indus and Indian society seem to share a class or caste system. The high-class Indian Brahmins (the priestly caste) may be like a modern Hindu version of the ancient Indus priest-rulers.

"Priest King" sculpture, Mohenjo-daro

Cleanliness and bathing

The idea of purification, which was so important to the Indus people, continues in the modern Hindu religion. One of the most sacred pilgrimages Hindus make is to bathe in the Ganges River.

Bathing at the Ganges

Jewelry

Modern Hindu bangles, necklaces, and nose ornaments look very like ancient Indus jewelry. Bangles are a particularly important way of showing a woman's status.

Boats

Local Pakistanis on the Indus River still use flat-bottomed ferryboats for their main river transportation, just like their ancestors did.

Indus seal

boat today

Bullock carts

Bullock carts are still used today near Mohenjo-daro. The modern designs sometimes include framed covers.

Indus figurine

cart today

Farming

Farmers use terracing to farm the hills around Islamabad in Pakistan, much as the ancient Indus farmers did. Many Indus crops and animals are still grown and raised by modern farmers in the area.

What happened to the Indus cities?

The Indus civilization fell into decay and collapsed in the centuries between 1900 and 1700 B.C.E. A number of things might have caused this...but no one knows for sure what it was.

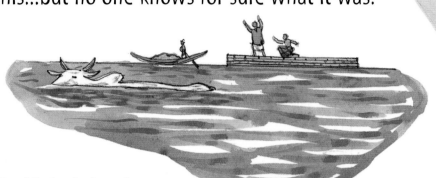

Could the Indus rivers have destroyed the civilization?

In the Indus area, rivers sometimes change their course and either dry up or flood. Such changes could have made farming impossible and caused major food shortages. There is evidence that Mohenjo-daro experienced several floods. Could there have been one huge flood which finally destroyed the city?

Could there have been an invasion?

In India's *Rig Veda* hymns (Hindu poems dating from about 1500 B.C.E.) there is mention of Aryan tribes destroying Indus cities. However, excavations don't back this story up because there is no evidence of widespread destruction. Also, the timing for the invasion mentioned in the hymns is wrong.

Were there earthquakes in the area?

Earthquakes could have caused flooding in parts of the Indus Valley, and destroyed Mohenjo-daro.

Mosquito

Could disease have ruined Indus city life?

Archeologists studying the skeletons at the Mohenjo-daro site have discovered that many people died from malaria, carried by mosquitoes, and other serious illnesses. There is even a suggestion that the waste from the city drains contaminated the well water and caused an outbreak of cholera. This would have killed a lot of people and perhaps made it impossible for others to survive.

Cholera bacterium

What do we know about life outside the cities?

Most Indus people were farmers who lived in rural areas. However, very little research has been done to find out what life outside the cities was like. Some of the surviving clay figurines are of rural people, and some villages and herdsmen's camps have been found, but this is the only evidence that has been analyzed. Work is now planned to find out more about the farming population.

Recently, a team of historians suspended a camera on a specially designed hot-air balloon which they floated over the Mohenjo-daro site. The camera took hundreds of aerial photographs which record all the remains in the city.

Dholavira

ARABIAN SEA

Dholavira is one of the most recent towns to be excavated.

What can we hope to find out in the future?

Since the big excavations in the 1920s, technology has advanced considerably. Work is being done today, with the most up-to-date techniques and equipment, to reassess the findings of past excavations. Through this work, and through new excavation work at other "town sites" and rural areas, archeologists hope to be able to answer some of the remaining questions, such as who ruled the civilization, how did they rule a huge area without an army, and what caused the collapse of the magnificent Indus civilization.

Timeline

6500-4000 B.C.E. Simple farming in what today is Northwest India and Pakistan. People use stone, copper, and bronze.

4000-3300 More farming settlements appear in the Indus area. They produce copper metalwork, fired wheel pottery, and beadwork.

3300 Harappa is a farming village near the Ravi River. Mohenjo-daro is a village on the Indus.

2800 Indus people begin to develop their own form of writing.

2600-2500 The full Indus civilization begins. It is a time of rapid change when craftsmanship and trade help the towns and cities develop.

2600-1900 The Indus civilization is at its height. There is city planning, writing, and trade with Mesopotamia.

2200 Harappa covers 370 acres (150ha). There were possibly as many as 80,000 people living there.

1900-1700 Trade and farming decline in the Indus area. Local cultures emerge. By 1600 the Indus culture reaches its end and is forgotten.

c. 1700 C.E. The British begin to rule India. Their colonial rule lasts until Indian independence, in 1947.

1800s The first Indus stamp seals are found but are not identified as part of an ancient civilization.

1920-21 The first excavations in Harappa and Mohenjo-daro take place, led by Sir John Marshall.

1948 Archeologist Sir Mortimer Wheeler excavates and finds early Indus pottery.

1986 Pakistanis and Americans carry out major digs in Harappa. They realize its population was far larger than previous estimates.

Today teams of international archeologists continue to excavate at Harappa, Dholavira, and elsewhere.

Glossary

archeologist
A person who digs up and studies the remains of buildings and objects from the past to find out about the people who made them.

artifacts
An object made by humans, such as a tool or a dish. The word is often used to describe objects of historical interest.

bitumen tar
A black, sticky, oil-based mud, found naturally in some areas. In Indus times, it was used to seal bricks together to make watertight buildings and wells.

citadel
An important area of a city, protected by walls. In Indus cities, the citadel is on a raised platform and contains religious and civic buildings. Unlike citadels in other parts of the world, Indus citadels do not seem to have been built to give people a safe place to hide if their city came under attack.

civic
If something is civic it is to do with a town or a city. For example, a town hall is a civic building.

excavate
To dig up an area of land in order to search for historical remains. An **excavation** is an archeological dig.

flint
A very hard stone that was often used in the past to make tools, such as axes and knives.

granary
Large building used for storing grain.

hearth
The floor of a fireplace, or a type of fireplace that is not built into a wall.

merchant
Someone who buys and sells or trades things. A merchant can also be called a trader.

seal
A small stone with a picture or writing carved on it. A seal is pushed into something soft, like clay or wax, to stamp the picture or writing into it. Seals were used in Indus times, mainly to record the buying and selling of goods.

trade routes
Pathways and roads used by traders and merchants to travel across land or water to sell their goods.

Index

archeologist 6, 7, 8, 9, 12, 14, 16, 17, 20, 21, 26, 27, 28, 29
artifact 9, 14, 22, 29

brick-making 18
builder 11, 18, 19

citadel 6, 8, 10, 16, 17, 18, 20, 21, 29
craftsman 7, 9, 12, 13, 14, 21, 28
Cunningham, Sir Alexander 8

Dholavira 8, 27, 28

farmer 12, 13, 17, 25, 27
farming 7, 10, 11, 13, 17, 25, 26, 27, 28
figurine 24, 25, 27

granary 17, 20, 29
Great Bath 10, 12, 16, 19, 20

Harappa 6, 7, 8, 9, 10, 11, 12, 15, 16, 24, 28
Hinduism 12, 24, 25
house 7, 17, 19, 21, 22, 23

India 6, 8, 12, 24, 26, 28
Indus city
    beginning of 6-7
    decline of 7, 26-27
    life in 20-21
    people of 6, 11, 12, 13, 14, 16, 21, 22, 23, 24, 26
    planning of 7, 16-17
Indus River 6, 7, 8, 10, 25, 28

jewelry 7, 12, 13, 14, 15, 21, 25, 26, 29

landowner 17, 20
lower city 6, 16, 17, 19, 21

Marshall, Sir John 8, 16, 28
merchant 7, 9, 17, 20, 29
Mesopotamia 11, 13, 14, 28
metalwork 14, 28
Mohenjo-daro 6, 7, 8, 10, 12, 15, 16, 17, 20, 24, 25, 26, 27, 28

Pakistan 6, 24, 25, 28
pottery 7, 8, 9, 12, 13, 14, 21, 28
priest 7, 13, 20, 24

Ravi River 8, 10, 11, 28
religion 7, 12, 13, 20, 24, 25

Sarasvati River 8, 10
sculpture 12, 24
seal 7, 8, 9, 12, 13, 14, 20, 21, 24, 25, 28, 29

tool 13, 18, 21, 22, 29
trade 7, 11, 13, 14, 15, 28
trader 7, 11, 13, 14, 15, 20, 29

water system 11, 19, 23, 26
women 12, 13
workshop 21, 22, 23
writing 12, 20, 28, 29